hors d'oeuvres

THIRD IN THE SERIES: *ANNIE'S ELEGANT, DELICIOUS COOKING*

annie simensen

PHOTOGRAPHY BY CARLA NARRETT

hors d'oeuvres

THIRD IN THE SERIES: *ANNIE'S ELEGANT, DELICIOUS COOKING*

Photography by: Carla Narrett

Book design, layout and image editing by Picturia Press (www.picturiapress.com)

Acknowledgements

MY HEARTFELT THANKS to my photographer, editor and friend, Carla Narrett, with gratitude and respect for her immense talent, organization skills and true friendship; to my husband, Jac, for supporting and encouraging my life-long adventure with food and cooking; and to my daughter, Jennifer Siemon, her husband CK and my grandchildren, Casey and Trevor for their years of taste testing and encouraging feedback.

Introduction

HORS D'OEUVRES is the third volume in the series *Annie's Elegant, Delicious, Cooking*. Like the first two volumes, *Salads* and *The Main Course*, *Hors d'Oeuvres* features a full page color photo with every easy-to-follow recipe to help you choose and prepare dishes that are both visually stunning and that appeal to your personal preferences and tastes. My straight-forward, time-tested recipes will enable cooks at all levels of experience to prepare mouthwateringly delicious dishes from ingredients that are readily available in American supermarkets. None of my recipes require special culinary training, equipment, expertise or complex processes.

Traditionally, hors d'oeuvres, (also called "appetizers" or "starters") were the first courses of a formal, sit-down dinner; their mission was to excite the senses and prepare diners for the varied flavors and textures of the dishes that would follow. Although today's relaxed lifestyles and dietary requirements seldom have room to accommodate six and seven course meals, hors d'oeuvres still hold an important place in both formal and informal entertaining – from the nuts, pretzels, chip-and-dip laid out in bowls on the kitchen counter, to the trays of finger-food passed by servers at a reception, to "heavy" hors d'oeuvres, (a combination of small plates served as a meal in itself), or later at the table as a first course - hors d'oeuvres span the full range of informal and formal dining and entertaining.

To make menu planning more convenient, I've organized the hors d'oeuvres recipes in this book into two groups:

 – *"No-cook" recipes but some assembly or preparation needed, and*
 – *Recipes requiring some cooking or baking*

A selection of several hors d'oeuvres plates from these groupings along with a bottle of wine and a salad, can create an informal lunch for a small group or a late dinner for two.

Like all of the easy-to-follow recipes in *Annie's Elegant, Delicious Cooking*, these hors d'oeuvres will turn out perfectly every time.

Contents

CHAPTER ONE

"NO-COOK" RECIPES BUT SOME ASSEMBLY OR PREPARATION NEEDED

Blue Brie Cheese Spread

I'm very partial to **all** types of blue cheese and here I'm using a flavorful but mellow one.

Ingredients

10 oz. round of "Saga" Blue Brie, softened at room temperature and cut into 1½ inch chunks

2 egg yolks

4 oz. (1 stick) unsalted butter, softened at room temperature

¼ cup heavy cream, not whipped

1 pinch ground cayenne pepper

To serve: lots of different crackers

Directions

1. Place all of the ingredients in the bowl of the stand mixer and mix until everything is well-blended. Use a rubber spatula to scrape down the sides when needed.

2. Place this in a glass or ceramic serving bowl or a 12 oz. capacity ramekin.

3. Cover with plastic wrap and place in the refrigerator for up to 24 hours.

4. Bring it out just when you're ready to serve it.

5. Place the bowl or ramekin on a large plate or cutting board and surround it with lots of different crackers and a knife for spreading.

Boursin Stuffed Mushrooms

These raw mushrooms are delicious and take very little preparation time.

Ingredients

8 – 12 oz. fresh Baby Bella mushrooms (Remove and discard the entire stem and wipe each mushroom with a damp paper towel.)

1- 6.5 oz. container of Boursin cheese

Directions

1. Place the Boursin in a pastry bag fitted with a large nozzle.

2. Pipe the cheese generously into each mushroom.

3. Place these on a platter or plate and serve.

 NOTE: If you would rather not use a pastry bag, you can spoon the cheese into the mushrooms.

"Caviar" Cream in Fillo Shells

This is an unusual way to serve "caviar". One of the great things about this recipe is that you don't have to make the fillo shells. You can fill these shells 1 hour before you need them. Keep them in the refrigerator. Delicious!

Ingredients

1 box frozen mini fillo shells (I use the Athens brand. There are 15 shells in the box.)

6 oz. heavy cream, whipped until quite stiff in the stand mixer with the balloon whisk attachment.

1 – 2 oz. jar lumpfish "caviar" (I use the Romanoff brand. You can usually find the lumpfish in red, yellow or black. I use the red for this. Please drain off the excess liquid.)

¼ teaspoon fresh lemon juice

¼ teaspoon salt

Directions

1. Place the 15 shells on a serving platter. There is no need to thaw these.

2. Add ½ the "caviar", lemon juice and salt to the whipped cream in the stand mixer. Mix on low speed just until blended. This won't take more than 5 seconds.

3. Spoon (or pipe with a large nozzle and pastry bag) the mixture into each cup.

4. Top each filled shell with a tiny bit of caviar.

Cheese Board

Cheese boards are fun to make because you get to choose just the cheeses that you particularly like. Here are the ones that I most often choose.

Ingredients

Brie

Mango coated Brillat-Savarin

Roquefort

Sharp Cheddar

To serve: Carr's water crackers and red and and green grapes.

Directions

1. Arrange the cheeses with the crackers and some grapes on a board, platter or twig "plate."

Cheese, Thyme and Garlic Dip for Crudités

This dip just bursts with flavor and can easily sit in the refrigerator, well covered, for 5 days. I serve this surrounded by raw Baby Bella mushrooms, crinkle slices of raw yellow squash and raw small zucchini, baby carrots, large red radishes and slices of red pepper.

Ingredients

8 oz. good cream cheese, not light or reduced fat, softened (I use the Philadelphia brand.)

⅔ cup sour cream, not light (I use Breakstone's.)

5 sprigs of fresh thyme (leaves should be pulled gently off the stems)

1 large clove of garlic, peeled and chopped very finely

¼ teaspoon kosher salt (Start with this amount. You may need more.)

⅛ teaspoon ground white pepper

To serve: fresh raw vegetables

Directions

1. In a stand mixer, blend all of the prepared dip ingredients together.

2. Transfer this to a pretty serving bowl and cover tightly with plastic wrap. Place in the refrigerator for up to 5 days.

3. When you are ready to serve, place the uncovered bowl of dip in the middle of a large round platter and surround it with the fresh, raw vegetables.

Crab Dip

This dip is always a great success at parties and it's so easy to make because all of the ingredients get mixed in the stand mixer. There is no cooking involved.

Ingredients

8 oz. good cream cheese, not light or reduced fat, softened (I use the Philadelphia brand.)

2 Tablespoons grated yellow onion (This will look like a watery paste.)

Juice from 1 lemon

1½ teaspoons grated horseradish (from a refrigerated jar)

3 Tablespoons good mayonnaise, not light (I use Hellman's.)

3 shakes Worcestershire sauce

3 shakes Tabasco hot sauce

1 – 16 oz. "see through can" of pasteurized crab meat, drained (This can be found in the fresh seafood department of your supermarket. It is already cooked.)

To serve: commercially baked bagel slices

Directions

1. Mix all of the ingredients, except for the crab, together in the bowl of your stand mixer. Mix just until well blended.

2. Now add the crab meat and mix slowly just until everything is well blended.

3. Transfer the dip to a serving dish and cover with plastic wrap and refrigerate for up to 24 hours.

4. I serve this with commercially baked bagel slices. (The Stacy's brand is good.)

Herb Cheese

I make a large quantity of this delicious filling because it freezes well. Using a pastry bag and a large nozzle, I fill cherry tomatoes, sugar snap peas and salami "cones" for an hors d'œuvres platter. This herb cheese can be melted and served over cooked vegetables and it's the best spread for cucumber sandwiches.

Ingredients

2 – 8 oz. packages cream cheese, not light or reduced fat, softened at room temperature and cut into 2 inch chunks (I use the Philadelphia brand.)

8 oz. butter, softened at room temperature

1 cup fresh basil leaves, washed and dried

¼ cup fresh oregano leaves, washed and dried

¼ cup fresh mint leaves, washed and dried

½ cup fresh flat leaved parsley, washed, dried and stems removed

8 cloves garlic, peeled

To serve: *thin slices of salami, cherry tomatoes and sugar snap peas.*

Directions

1. Place the herbs and garlic in the food processor and pulse until everything looks well blended. Scrape down the sides with a rubber spatula.

2. Add the chunks of cream cheese and softened butter and process until all ingredients are mixed together.

3. Place a portion of this herb cheese in a pastry bag fitted with a tube that has a large fluted opening. Fill the vegetables and salami "cones" and arrange everything on a large platter.

4. Freeze what you don't use now in small, 2 oz. capacity ramekins. Cover each portion with 2 layers of plastic wrap.

Hors d'Oeuvres Platter

Get out a large rectangular platter or cutting board and fill it with the following four things. This is the way to go when you don't have the time to make an hors d'œuvres from scratch.

Ingredients

Pitted Kalamata olives

Chunks of your favorite cheese

Wedges of peeled and deseeded cantaloupe wrapped in very thin slices of prosciutto

6 inch long bamboo skewers with mozzarella balls, basil leaves and small "grape" tomatoes

Hummus

Hummus can be bought ready-made, but the difference between that and this homemade version is significant.

This hummus can be made 3 days in advance of when you need it. Just keep it well covered with plastic wrap in the refrigerator. This can also be frozen successfully.

Ingredients

2 – 15.5 oz. cans chickpeas (garbanzo beans) drained and rinsed

4 cloves garlic, peeled

⅔ cup tahini paste (Use the one that comes in a jar in the international section of your supermarket.)

Juice of 2 large limes (⅓ to ½ cup)

4 Tablespoons extra virgin olive oil

⅛ teaspoon ground cayenne pepper

1 teaspoon salt

½ teaspoon freshly ground pepper

¾ teaspoon sesame oil (NO MORE!)

4 Tablespoons water

To serve: your favorite bagel or pita chips or raw vegetables

Directions

1. Place all of the ingredients in the food processor and process until smooth. If you feel this is too thick, just add some more olive oil.

2. Place in an 8 inch square by 2 inch high serving dish.

3. Sprinkle a little more ground cayenne pepper and a little more olive oil over the top.

4. Serve with bagel or pita chips and raw vegetables.

Marinated Rounds of Goat Cheese

This is the best way to bring out the super flavor of goat cheese. These marinated rounds can be used in salads, broiled on French bread slices or served plain with crackers.

Ingredients

1 lb. plain goat cheese (no rind), cut into 16 even slices*

6 – 3 inch long stems of fresh rosemary

6 stems fresh thyme

4 large cloves of garlic, peeled

1 Tablespoon crushed, dried red pepper flakes

1 Tablespoon peppercorns, any color, not crushed or ground

2 whole dried bay leaves

2½ cups extra virgin olive oil

Directions

1. Place all ingredients in a 6 cup capacity glass bowl and cover tightly with plastic wrap.

2. Let the bowl sit in the refrigerator for at least 1 day to allow the cheese to absorb all of the flavors.

3. As long as the cheese is covered by the oil, it will keep in the refrigerator for 2 weeks.

 NOTE: It's best not to use a knife to cut the cheese. Just use a clean thin wire. Each slice will be 1/3 inch thick.

My Favorite Guacamole

This is actually 2 recipes. If you don't want the guacamole right now, just eliminate the avocados and the rest of the ingredients make a really super salsa which can be served with scrambled eggs or tortilla chips.

Ingredients

3 ripe Haas avocados, peeled, pitted, quartered and dipped in the juice of 1 lime.

4 cloves garlic, peeled

6 – 8 scallions, derooted, washed and cut into 1 inch pieces. (Use all of the white part and 5 inches of the green part.)

2 Campari tomatoes, washed and quartered

4 slices pickled jalapeno peppers from a jar

3 Tablespoons fresh cilantro leaves

½ teaspoon salt and 8 grinds peppercorns

To serve: *tortilla chips*

Directions

1. Place all of the ingredients in the food processor and process until quite smooth. Scrape down the sides a few times with a rubber spatula.

2. Place the guacamole in a glass or ceramic serving dish. Press a piece of plastic wrap directly on top of the guacamole and place in the refrigerator until you need it.

3. Serve this with your favorite brand of tortilla chips.

 NOTE: Haas avocados are usually grown in Mexico. The flesh is dense and full of flavor. When you buy them, make sure that the skin is black and that the whole avocado "gives" a bit when you gently pinch it. The large light green avocados that are grown in Florida do not have as much flavor as the Haas variety and the flesh can be watery, instead of dense.

Pantry Hors d'Oeuvres

This is definitely the direction to go when you have last minute guests for drinks. All of these items can sit unopened in your pantry shelves for weeks! These are my favorite brands. Feel free to use what you like.

Ingredients

Whole cashews

"Bella" oil cured black olives

"Ka-me" rice crackers

"Vigo" Greek Pepperoncini

"Mezzetta" garlic stuffed olives

"Planters" honey roasted peanuts

"Cape Cod" kettle- cooked potato chips

"Blue Diamond" smokehouse almonds

"Southwestern Spices" Tostitos tortilla chips

"Tostitos" roasted garlic, thick and chunky salsa

"Snyder's of Hanover" pretzels

Pesto and Goat Cheese Spread

This spread is really packed full of flavor. I use it 2 ways: as a spread for crackers and as a sandwich spread instead of using mayonnaise.

Ingredients

5 oz. goat cheese, softened

3 oz. good quality cream cheese, softened (I use the Philadelphia brand, but not low-fat.)

⅔ cup pesto sauce, commercially made or homemade (This recipe can be found in one of my earlier cookbooks, The Main Course, on page 116.)

Salt and pepper, only if you want it

To serve: assorted crackers

Directions

1. Blend the first 3 ingredients together in a stand mixer. Now taste to see if you want a little salt or pepper or both.

2. Pack the spread in a 12 oz. ramekin. Cover with plastic wrap and keep it in the refrigerator.

3. Serve this with your favorite crackers.

Sausage, Olive and Bread Platter

This is the way to go when you have no time to prepare an hors d'œuvres from scratch.

Ingredients

3 different types of whole smoked sausages

1 loaf of unsliced artisan bread

Butter

1 dish of olives

Directions

1. Arrange everything on a large wooden cutting board.

Smoked Salmon Slices with Brown Bread and Boursin

There is no cooking needed to put this beautiful platter on the table.

Ingredients

8 oz. pre-sliced vacuumed packed smoked salmon

6 slices brown bread, crusts removed and cut diagonally in half

1 – 6.5 oz. container of Boursin cheese

¼ red onion, peeled and very thinly sliced

GARNISH:

Sprigs of fresh dill and wedges of fresh lemons and limes

Directions

1. Get out a platter and roll the slices of smoked salmon. Place them in a row down the middle of the platter.

2. Spread the triangles of brown bread evenly with the Boursin and arrange them on a plate next to the salmon.

3. Arrange the very thinly sliced red onion on either side of the salmon.

4. Place a few sprigs of fresh dill along side of the salmon.

5. Place a few wedges of lemon and lime around the edge of the platter.

Smoked Salmon Spread

I make this recipe all the time for a beginning to a dinner or for an addition to a big brunch.

Ingredients

10 oz. smoked salmon, pre-sliced

4 oz. (1 stick) unsalted butter, softened (plus 2 oz. for buttering the bread)

¾ cup crème fraiche (in the dairy section of your supermarket)

Juice and zest of 1 lemon

1 pinch ground cayenne pepper

1 pinch ground white pepper

Salt, to taste

GARNISH:

thin slices of lemons, deseeded, and a few sprigs of fresh parsley.

To serve: 12 slices crustless brown bread, not dark pumpernickel, buttered and cut in half on the diagonal.

Directions

1. Mix the first 6 ingredients together, except for the 2 oz. of butter, in the food processor until well blended. You may have to scrape the sides down with a rubber spatula a few times.

2. Now taste the spread to see if you want to add salt. Sometimes the smoked salmon is salty enough.

3. Pack the spread in a 2 cup (16 oz.) capacity serving dish. Decorate with the garnishes.

4. Place this dish in the center of a large round platter.

5. Place the buttered bread triangles around the spread. Serve with a knife on the side.

CHAPTER TWO

REQUIRING SOME COOKING OR BAKING

Baked Chiles Rellenos

This dish is very delicious and extremely easy to make. I serve it either as an hors d'œuvres or as a brunch dish. It is made in a glass 9 inch by 13 inch baking dish.

Ingredients

3 – 4 oz. cans roasted, peeled and seeded mild green chili peppers

½ pound grated Cheddar cheese (I buy this ready- grated in a plastic bag.)

½ pound grated Monterey Jack cheese (I buy this ready- grated in a plastic bag.)

1¾ cups whole fresh milk

4 large eggs

⅓ cup all purpose flour

1 teaspoon salt

To serve on the side: *ready-made salsa in a bowl and sour cream in a bowl.*

Directions

1. Preheat your oven to 350°F and lightly oil a 9 inch by 13 inch glass baking dish (such as Pyrex).

2. Each can of chili peppers will contain 3 whole peppers. Split each one down 1 side with a sharp knife and lay flat on paper towels to drain. Place all of the chili peppers evenly on the bottom of the pan. Now evenly sprinkle all of the grated cheddar cheese and the grated jack cheese over the chili peppers.

3. In a blender, mix the milk, eggs, flour and salt for 10 seconds.

4. Pour this mixture evenly over the chili peppers and the cheese.

5. Bake at 350°F for 38 to 40 minutes. The top will look dark golden brown and the center will not move when slightly shaken.

6. Remove from the oven and let cool for 5 to 10 minutes.

7. Cut into small squares and serve with the salsa of your choice and sour cream on the side.

Broiled Shrimp and Bacon

This is a delicious way to serve shrimp. I use this as an hors d'œuvres and sometimes as the "Surf" portion of a "Surf and Turf" entrée.

Ingredients

12 frozen raw jumbo shrimp

3 strips of bacon, each sliced into fourths

¼ cup soy sauce (I use Kikkoman)

Directions

1. Place the shrimp in boiling water for 2 minutes. Now peel each shrimp and cut down the back with a sharp knife to remove the orange or black intestine.

2. Dry each shrimp with a paper towel.

3. Wrap each piece of bacon around each shrimp and secure the bacon with 1 or 2 toothpicks.

4. Dip each prepared shrimp quickly into the soy sauce. (A little goes a long way!)

5. Preheat your broiler.

6. Spread all of the prepared shrimp in 1 layer on an oven broiling pan.

7. Broil for 2 minutes.

8. Now turn each one over and broil for 1 more minute.

9. Place the shrimp on a plate and serve warm.

Broiled Vegetables with Yogurt and Cucumber Sauce

This dish looks beautiful and is amazingly delicious.

Ingredients

3 small zucchini, stems removed and sliced thinly lengthwise

3 small yellow squash, stems removed and sliced thinly lengthwise

2 very small eggplants, stems removed and sliced thinly lengthwise

1 green bell pepper, 1 red bell pepper and 1 yellow bell pepper, stem and insides removed and cut in half lengthwise

3 Tablespoons extra virgin olive oil

SAUCE:

½ European (hot house) cucumber, unpeeled and grated in the food processor

¼ cup sour cream (not light)

1 cup plain Greek yogurt (not light)

1 Tablespoon white wine vinegar

1 Tablespoon fresh lemon juice

1 ½ Tablespoons fresh dill, stems removed and chopped finely in the mini food processor

2 cloves garlic, peeled and chopped finely in the mini food processor

A pinch of freshly ground pepper and salt

Directions

1. Preheat your broiler and get out 3 cookie sheets with sides.

2. Place all of the prepared peppers on 1 cookie sheet, brush them with the extra virgin olive oil and broil them until the skins look quite black. Remove them from the oven and place them in a sealed Ziploc bag for 10 minutes. When you remove them, the skins will peel off quickly.

3. Place the other prepared vegetables on the next 2 cookie sheets and brush each slice with extra virgin olive oil. Broil these until they are tender.

4. While these are broiling, mix all of the sauce ingredients together in a glass or ceramic bowl.

5. Arrange all of the vegetables on a platter with a bowl of the sauce on the side.

Cheddar Crackers

These crackers are so easy to make in a stand mixer and they freeze extremely well. I try to always have a supply of them to serve with drinks.

Ingredients

1 lb. grated extra sharp cheddar cheese (I use the ready grated that comes in a bag in the refrigerated cheese section of the supermarket.)

½ lb. (8 oz.) butter, softened at room temperature

2 cups all-purpose flour

½ teaspoon cayenne pepper

Directions

1. In a stand mixer, cream the cheese and softened butter together until well mixed.

2. Add the flour gradually and then the cayenne pepper until the dough is well blended.

3. Shape this dough into 4 equal sized logs. Wrap each log in plastic wrap and refrigerate for 2 hours.

4. When you take the logs out of the refrigerator, turn your oven on to 400° F.

5. Unwrap the logs and cut each one into ⅓ inch slices.

6. Place these crackers 1 inch apart on Teflon coated cookie sheets.

7. Bake at 400° F for 8 to 9 minutes, until the top of each cracker is medium to dark golden brown.

 NOTE: This recipe will yield between 48 and 65 crackers.

Crab Meat and Cheddar Cheese Toasts

The combination of crab meat, cheddar and curry is unbeatable.

Ingredients

15 slices dense white bread (I use Pepperidge Farm.) Please remove the crusts and cut each slice into 3 rectangles.

8 oz. "see through can" of pasteurized crab meat, drained (This can be found in the fresh seafood department of your supermarket. It is already cooked.)

½ small onion, peeled and grated to a pulp

1 cup grated cheddar cheese

1 cup good quality mayonnaise, not light (I use Hellman's.)

1 teaspoon curry powder (no more, please)

½ teaspoon salt

Directions

1. Place the rectangles of bread on 2 Teflon coated cookie sheets.

2. Preheat your oven to BROIL.

3. Place the cookie sheets, 1 at a time, under the broiler for 1 minute or less, just until bread looks slightly golden. Repeat with 2nd cookie sheet.

4. Now turn all of these pieces over.

5. In a medium sized glass bowl, mix the crab meat, onion pulp, grated cheddar cheese, mayonnaise, curry powder and salt together gently. Spread onto the rectangles.

6. Now place the sheets, one at a time, under the broiler until the tops are golden and a little bubbly.

7. Place these on a platter or on an electric warming tray.

Crustless Bacon, Cheese and Onion Quiche

This is very delicious and also easy to make. I bake this in a Pyrex 9 inch in diameter deep-dish pie plate.

Ingredients

6 slices bacon, cooked until quite crisp and drained on paper towels. Reserve the grease to sauté the onions.

1 medium-sized yellow onion, peeled and sliced very thinly

¾ lb. (12 oz.) shredded Gruyère cheese

4 large eggs

2 cups heavy cream

¾ teaspoon salt

¼ teaspoon ground white pepper

1 pinch ground nutmeg

Directions

1. Preheat your oven to 425° F

2. Sauté the onions in the reserved bacon grease for 6 minutes or until completely tender.

3. Break the bacon slices into 1 inch pieces. Sprinkle the bacon pieces evenly on the bottom of the pie plate.

4. Now sprinkle the sautéed onions evenly over the bacon pieces.

5. Now sprinkle the grated Gruyère over the sautéed onions.

6. In a stand mixer or a blender, mix the eggs, cream, salt, white pepper and nutmeg together.

7. Pour this mixture slowly and evenly into the pie plate.

8. Place the pie plate on a cookie sheet with sides and bake for 10 minutes at 425° F. Then reduce the heat to 350° F and bake for 35 minutes more. (Quiche will be brown on top and a bit shaky in the middle when done.)

Curried Spiced Nuts

These nuts are so delicious and so easy to make. You can make them up to 2 weeks in advance. When they're completely cooled, store them in an airtight Ziploc bag. I like to serve them warm with pre-dinner drinks, so I just put the amount that I need in the microwave for 45 seconds.

Ingredients

1½ cups whole cashews

1½ cups pecan halves

1½ cups whole almonds

6 Tablespoons (3 oz.) melted butter

1 Tablespoon kosher salt

1 Tablespoon curry powder

Directions

1. Preheat your oven to 350° F.

2. Place all of the nuts in a 9" by 13" glass baking dish (such as Pyrex).

3. Mix the melted butter, salt and curry powder together in a small bowl.

4. Pour this mixture over the nuts and stir to coat evenly.

5. Bake for 6 minutes. Remove from the oven and stir. Bake for another 6 minutes. Remove from the oven and stir. Bake for 4 more minutes and remove from the oven.

6. You can serve them now while they're warm, or cool them completely and store them for use in the future.

 NOTE: Sometimes I make this recipe using 4½ cups of only pecan halves.

Curried Yogurt Dip

This is so easy to make and the flavor is "out of this world".

Ingredients

1½ cups plain, good quality yogurt (Yes, you can use Greek.)

20 fresh coriander leaves, chopped finely in the mini food processor

10 fresh mint leaves, chopped finely in the mini food processor

Zest of 1 whole lemon

1 Tablespoon curry powder, sautéed quickly in a sauté pan over medium heat to release maximum flavor.

To serve: *commercially made pita chips*

Directions

1. Stir all of the ingredients together (except the pita chips) in a medium sized glass bowl. Cover with plastic wrap and place in the refrigerator for at least one hour for the flavors to develop.

2. Serve this in a pretty bowl with lots of pita chips on the side.

Garlic and Anchovy Toasts

These toasts are full of flavor and can be made in advance. They are great with all Italian dishes. If you have any leftovers, use them as croutons in a green salad.

Ingredients

1 – 2 oz. can flat anchovy fillets, drained and chopped in the mini food processor

3 large cloves garlic, peeled and finely chopped in the mini food processor

4 Tablespoons extra virgin olive oil

6 slices dense white sandwich bread, crusts removed

Directions

1. Preheat your oven to 400° F and get out a Teflon coated cookie sheet.

2. Cut each slice of bread into 3 rectangles and place them in 1 layer on the cookie sheet.

3. In a small glass bowl, mix the prepared anchovies and garlic with the extra virgin olive oil .

4. Lightly spread this mixture on both sides of the 18 rectangles.

5. Bake for 3 minutes on one side, then turn them over and bake them for 3 more minutes.

6. You can serve these now, or cool them and store them in a Ziploc bag for up to 10 days.

Gruyère Tarts

I like to make these wonderful tarts in advance and keep them in the freezer. They can be used as an hors d'oeuvres or as a lunch with an added salad. I use 8 loose-bottomed tart tins which are 3 ½ inches in diameter.

Ingredients

1 box pre-made pie crusts (I use the Pillsbury brand. There will be 2 pie crusts in each box and can be found in the refrigerated section of your supermarket.)

2 large eggs

1 cup (8 oz.) heavy cream

½ teaspoon salt

¼ teaspoon ground white pepper

Pinch of grated nutmeg

1 Tablespoon Tabasco Sauce

8 oz. grated Gruyère

Directions

1. Preheat your oven to 375° F.

2. Cut out 8 – 5 inch in diameter circles from the box of pie crusts. You will get 4 circles from each of the pie crusts.

3. Line each tin with a circle of pie crust. Prick each crust all over with the tines of a fork.

4. Place the tart tins on 2 cookie sheets with sides and bake them without the filling for 7 minutes.

5. While these are baking, place the eggs, heavy cream, salt, pepper, grated nutmeg and Tabasco in a blender and mix until well blended.

6. When you remove the tart shells from the oven, evenly sprinkle the grated Gruyère over the pastries.

7. Now evenly pour the mixture from the blender into each tart shell.

8. Place the 2 cookie sheets with the tarts back in the 375° F oven for 16 minutes.

 NOTES: When they are finished, they should look medium golden brown on top. When they are cooled, you can remove the sides of the tins.

Hot Artichoke, Spinach and Parmesan Dip with Toasted Pita Chips

This hot dip has always been extremely popular. The combination of artichoke hearts, spinach and cheese is particularly delicious.

Ingredients

2 – 14 oz. cans artichoke hearts, drained and cut into ½ inch chunks

1 – 10 oz. package frozen chopped spinach, thawed and well drained. (I use Birds' Eye.)

½ cup sour cream, not light or reduced fat (I use Breakstone's.)

½ cup good quality mayonnaise (I use Hellman's.)

1 cup freshly grated Parmesan Cheese

1 cup shredded Jack cheese

6 "loaves" onion pita bread (6½ inches in diameter for each)

1½ Tablespoons extra virgin olive oil

2 teaspoons Lawry's garlic salt

Directions

1. Preheat your oven to 375°F.

2. Mix the first 5 prepared ingredients together in a medium sized glass bowl.

3. Transfer this mixture to a 6 cup capacity glass or ceramic baking dish. (I use the 7" by 11" Le Creuset gratin dish.)

4. Sprinkle the shredded Jack cheese evenly over the top.

5. Bake for 18 minutes at 375°F until bubbly around the edges.

6. While this is baking, place the pita "loaves" on 2 cookie sheets with sides. Drizzle a little extra virgin olive oil on both sides of each pita loaf. Now sprinkle some Lawry's garlic salt evenly over each side of the pita bread.

7. After the dip has baked and has been removed from the oven, turn the oven temperature to "Broil". Now slide the cookie sheets with the pita bread in the broiler for 1½ – 2 minutes on each side, until somewhat crisp, but not overly browned.

8. Cut each pita into 6 equal wedges and serve with the hot dip.

Hot Chicken Wings

This is an incredibly easy hors d'œuvres which doubles as a light supper if you add a salad and a loaf of artisan bread and good butter.

Ingredients

18 – 24 chicken wings (I prefer the Perdue brand.) Use them whole. You don't have to cut them into pieces. Just spread each one out as far as it will go.

Salt and pepper

½ lb. butter, melted

¾ cup (6 oz.) hot sauce (either Tabasco or Franks)

Directions

1. Preheat your oven to 375° F and get out 2 – 9" by 13" glass baking dishes (such as Pyrex).

2. Mix the butter and hot sauce together.

3. Place the wings in the 2 pans and sprinkle them lightly with salt and pepper.

4. Pour the butter mixture evenly over the wings.

5. Bake for 1 hour until the wings are golden brown.

 NOTES: You can serve these alone or with a good quality commercially made ranch dressing. After the leftovers (if you have any) are cooled, just place them in a Ziploc bag and freeze.

Liverwurst Spread

This is addictive and tastes so much better than most store bought pâtés.

Ingredients

5 medium-sized Baby Bella mushrooms, stems removed, wiped with a damp paper towel and sliced. If you place the mushrooms under running water they will absorb too much moisture and this will greatly alter the consistency of this spread.

1½ Tablespoons butter

½ lb. (8 oz.) best quality liverwurst, softened at room temperature and cut into chunks (I use the regular Boar's Head brand, not low sodium).

3 oz. good quality cream cheese, softened at room temperature (I use the Philadelphia brand, but not light or reduced fat.)

2 teaspoons Worcestershire sauce

½ teaspoon fresh thyme leaves (no stems)

¼ cup heavy cream, not whipped

4 grinds black peppercorns

1 Tablespoon green peppercorns packed in water, drained

To serve: bagel crisps and crackers

Directions

1. Sauté the sliced mushrooms in the butter over medium heat for 5 – 7 minutes until cooked, but not brown. Drain off excess liquid.

2. Transfer these mushrooms and all of the other ingredients to the food processor and blend well.

3. Pack into 3 - ½ cup capacity ramekins and cover tightly with plastic wrap. Keep in the refrigerator and use within 3 days. The flavors will continue to develop. If you don't need all 3 ramekins right now, just wrap the ones that you don't need tightly with plastic wrap and freeze them.

4. Serve with bagel crisps (The New York Style brand is very good.) I also serve the Carr's Cheese Melts with this, but please use YOUR favorite crackers.

Marinated Mushrooms

These mushrooms have a delicious fresh flavor and can be served by themselves for an hors d'œuvres. They also make a super addition to green salads.

Ingredients

1 lb. (16oz.) small fresh white button mushrooms (about 26)

MARINADE:

½ cup water

⅔ cup extra virgin olive oil

Juice and zest of 2 lemons

3 bay leaves

3 cloves garlic, peeled

5 peppercorns, any color

1 teaspoon salt

Directions

1. Bring all of the marinade ingredients to a boil in a large saucepan.

2. Turn the heat down and simmer the marinade for 10 minutes, uncovered.

3. While the marinade is simmering, wipe each mushroom with a damp paper towel and cut off the stem. Leave the mushrooms whole.

4. Strain the marinade and return it to the pan. Dispose of the solids.

5. Add the prepared mushrooms to the pan and simmer them uncovered for 7 minutes. Taste one to see if it's tender.

6. Let the mushrooms cool to room temperature in the marinade. Do not drain.

7. Place the mushrooms and the marinade in a glass dish with a lid and refrigerate for up to 4 days.

Mussels in Garlic Sauce

This is the most delicious way to serve fresh mussels. Make sure you have a baguette torn into big chunks to soak up the sauce.

Ingredients

3 dozen fresh mussels in their shells

3 Tablespoons extra virgin olive oil

7 scallions (Cut off the roots, wash and use all of the white part and 5 inches of the green part. Cut into 1 inch long pieces and chop finely in the food processor.)

7 cloves garlic, peeled and chopped finely in the food processor

1 Tablespoon flour

1 cup dry white wine

1 bay leaf

2 Tablespoons fresh lemon juice

½ teaspoon salt

¼ teaspoon ground black pepper

GARNISH:

finely chopped fresh parsley

Directions

1. Scrub the mussels under cold running water and remove the "beard" which is usually attached to the shell. DISCARD ANY MUSSELS THAT ARE OPEN.

2. In a 12 inch heavy bottomed sauté pan, sauté the prepared scallions and garlic in the extra virgin olive oil over medium heat until tender. This will take about 3 minutes.

3. Stir in the flour and cook for 1 minute.

4. Add the wine, bay leaf, lemon juice, salt and pepper.

5. Cover the pan and simmer for 5 minutes.

6. Now add the prepared mussels to the sauce.

7. Cover and simmer for about 3 minutes until the mussels have opened.

8. DISCARD ANY MUSSELS WHICH HAVE NOT OPENED.

9. Place the mussels and the sauce in a large serving bowl and sprinkle some parsley over the top.

Roasted Shrimp Cocktail

Roasting shrimp, instead of boiling the shrimp in water, will give you a better taste for this particular recipe. And this presentation is not at all difficult, but the visual effect is great.

Ingredients

1 lb. frozen raw jumbo shrimp

1 Tablespoon extra virgin olive oil

Salt and pepper to taste

COCKTAIL SAUCE:

1 ½ cups good quality ketchup (I use Heinz.)

2 Tablespoons grated horseradish (This can be found in jars in the refrigerator section of your supermarket.)

1 Tablespoon fresh lime juice

1 Tablespoon Worcestershire sauce

1 teaspoon dried mustard (I use the Coleman's brand.)

½ teaspoon ground peppercorns

1 Tablespoon Tabasco hot sauce

GARNISH:

Washed and dried leaves of Boston lettuce

Slices of lime

Directions

1. Preheat your oven to 400° F.

2. Thaw the shrimp quickly under warm water. Pat them dry and peel most of the shell off. Just leave the small amount of shell on the tail. Make a slit along the back of each shrimp and remove the orange or black intestine.

3. Spread the shrimp out evenly on a Teflon coated cookie sheets with sides and evenly sprinkle the extra virgin olive oil and the salt and pepper over the top.

4. Roast the shrimp in the preheated oven for 3 minutes. Now turn each one over and roast for 3 more minutes, until just cooked through.

5. While the shrimp is in the oven, mix all of the cocktail sauce ingredients together in a glass or ceramic bowl.

6. Spoon some of the sauce in the bottom of martini glasses.

7. Place 1 or 2 lettuce leaves in each glass.

8. Place the roasted shrimp on the edge of the glasses. Add a thin slice of lime.

9. Serve these now or cover them with plastic wrap and put them in the refrigerator until you are ready to serve.

Sautéed Panko Coated Goat Cheese Rounds

The taste of warm goat cheese is sensational. If you prefer, you could skip the taco sauce and serve the breaded rounds of goat cheese on individual beds of "spring mix" fresh greens.

Ingredients

12 oz. vacuumed packed French goat cheese

3 eggs mixed with 1 Tablespoon extra virgin olive oil and 1 teaspoon salt

2½ cups unflavored Panko crumbs

3 Tablespoons butter

3 Tablespoons extra virgin olive oil

1 cup (8 oz.) medium hot taco sauce

GARNISH:

leaves of Bibb lettuce

Directions

1. Slice the cheese into 12 equal sized rounds. Use a clean thin wire for this, not a knife.

2. Dip each round into the egg mixture, then into the Panko crumbs. Press the crumbs firmly around the cheese. Place these on a cookie sheet and refrigerate for ½ hour.

3. Combine the butter and extra virgin olive oil in a large skillet over medium heat. Place the rounds in the skillet and sauté 2 minutes on <u>each</u> side until golden brown.

4. Place taco sauce in small ramekins.

5. Place sautéed rounds on pieces of Bibb lettuce on a platter surrounded by the ramekins.

Shrimp Spread

This spread is rich and very delicious. It will easily keep in the refrigerator, covered, for 2 days.

Ingredients

1¼ pound frozen raw shrimp, medium to large sized, simmered in hot water for 4 minutes until cooked through, then peeled, deveined*and tail removed.

7 scallions, derooted, washed and cut into 1 inch pieces. (Only use the white part and 3 inches of the green part.)

4 oz. (or 1 stick) butter, room temperature

⅓ cup good quality mayonnaise, not light (I use Hellman's.)

⅓ cup heavy cream, not whipped

Zest and juice of 1 lime

Salt and ground white pepper to taste

To serve: Buttered, crustless brown bread slices (not pumpernickel). Cut the slices diagonally in half.

Directions

1. Place the first 6 prepared ingredients in the food processor and process until the mixture looks smooth. Scrape down the sides with the spatula and taste to see how much salt and pepper you want.

2. Pack this into a 3 – 4 cup capacity shallow serving bowl.

3. Serve with the buttered bread triangles.

 **NOTE:** After you have peeled the cooked shrimp, cut down the back with a sharp serrated knife and remove the black or orange intestine.

Spinach, Pine Nut and Onion Tart

This is a truly delicious hors d'œuvres. I also serve it for lunch or for a light supper. Use the pre-made pie pastry in the dairy section of your supermarket.

Ingredients

1 pre-made pie pastry (I use Pillsbury.)

3 Tablespoons butter

1 medium sized yellow onion, peeled and very thinly sliced

1 – 10 oz. package frozen chopped spinach (I use Bird's Eye.) Please thaw the spinach and drain it well.

4 large eggs

1½ cups heavy cream, not whipped

1 teaspoon salt

¼ teaspoon black or white pepper

1 pinch nutmeg

3 Tablespoons pine nuts, lightly toasted in a small frying pan

4 Tablespoons freshly grated Parmesan cheese

Directions

Preheat oven to 400°F.

1. This can be done ahead of time. Roll out the pastry to 12 inches in diameter. Line a 9 inch loose bottomed Teflon-coated tart pan with the pastry. Prick the pastry all over the sides and bottom with the tines of a fork. Now gently lay a piece of foil on top of the pastry and fill the shell either with uncooked rice or uncooked beans. Place the tart pan on a cookie sheet with sides. Bake at 400° F for 10 minutes. Then remove the foil and rice or beans and continue baking for 7 more minutes. Remove from the oven and fill with the filling when you are ready.

2. Now reduce the oven temperature to 350° F.

3. Melt the butter in a large skillet and cook the sliced onions for about 10 minutes over medium heat until tender, but not browned. Stir this often and when it's completely tender stir in the prepared spinach.

4. In a blender or a medium-sized glass bowl, mix the eggs, cream, salt, pepper and nutmeg together.

5. Place the spinach and onion mixture into the prepared baked pastry shell.

6. Pour the egg mixture evenly on top of the spinach and onion mixture.

7. Now evenly sprinkle the pine nuts and grated Parmesan over the top of the tart.

8. Place the prepared tart on a cookie sheet with sides and bake for 45 minutes. Remove from the oven while the tart is still a little bit shaky in the middle. Let sit for 10 minutes.

The Way I Serve "Caviar"

I line a 10 inch quiche dish with chopped hard boiled eggs mixed with melted butter and fill the pan with sour cream and chopped scallions. At the last minute I place 2 different colors of lumpfish roe in the middle. This is beautiful and very delicious.

Ingredients

10 large hard boiled eggs, peeled and chopped

½ cup (4 oz.) melted butter

2 cups (16 oz.) good quality sour cream, not light (I use Breakstone's.)

14 scallions, washed, derooted and sliced thinly. Use all of the white part and 3 inches of the green part.

2 – 2 oz. jars of "Romanoff" lumpfish roe. (1 jar of red and 1 jar of yellow)

Directions

1. Get out a 10 inch in diameter glass or ceramic quiche pan.

2. In a large bowl, mix the chopped eggs and the butter together.

3. Press this mixture evenly on the bottom and the sides of the quiche pan.

4. Spread 2 cups of the sour cream evenly over the egg mixture. Please leave some egg showing all around the outside border.

5. Sprinkle the chopped scallions evenly in a circle around the outer edge of the sour cream.

6. Place the dish in the refrigerator until you are ready to serve.

7. When you are ready, spoon the "caviar" on top of the sour cream.

8. Cut this into wedges and serve on small plates.

Toasted Blue Cheese Baguette Slices

You can make these toasts while everyone is standing around talking and having drinks. They are particularly good when they are warm.

Ingredients

1 – 20 inch long fresh baguette, slice diagonally into 10 or 12 - ½ inch thick slices

3 Tablespoons extra virgin olive oil

6 oz. good quality blue cheese, softened (I like Rosenborg Danish.)

4 Tablespoons sour cream, not light or reduced fat (I use Breakstone's.)

Directions

1. Preheat your oven to 375° F and get out a cookie sheet with sides; preferably Teflon-coated.

2. In a medium-sized glass bowl, mix the cheese together with the sour cream.

3. Place the slices of bread on the cookie sheet and brush both sides with the extra virgin olive oil.

4. Bake for 4 minutes, then turn and bake for 2 minutes more.

5. Spread the cheese mixture evenly on the toasts and bake for 2 – 3 minutes more until the cheese has melted.

About the Author

ANNIE SIMENSEN has spent much of her life in kitchens: kitchens in the twenty-two homes and apartments around the world she's shared with her husband and daughter, and kitchens in schools where she honed her culinary technique and expertise with some of the top European and Asian instructors and chefs.

After graduating from college with a degree in education, Annie married her college sweetheart who was developing a complementary passion for fine wine. They regularly vacationed in Europe and enthusiastically explored regional cuisines and wines, more often in bistros and cafes than in 'starred' restaurants. From these experiences, Annie began to experiment with dishes not then common in American homes: squid cooked in its own ink, garlic roasted quail, and slow, oven-roasted goose. Then, she began the process of developing recipes of her own creation, which, over the years, evolved into this series of cookbooks, *Annie's Elegant, Delicious Cooking*.

In the late seventies Annie's husband went to work for a British company; the family moved to England and began what would become an eighteen year journey around the world. In the little village of South Ascot, Annie befriended a woman who had, for most of her life, been 'in service' in the kitchen of a Royal household. Under her tutelage, Annie discovered how to make perfect 'Yorkshire Pudding,' how to operate a 'tongue press,' and was entrusted with the private recipe for the Duchess of Windsor's favorite chocolate dessert.

After finishing several single topic courses at Le Cordon Bleu cooking school in London, Annie decided to enroll in the Cordon Bleu certificate course, the intensive course that prepares students for careers in the restaurant and food business. The course was both physically and academically demanding, but she passed the hands-on and written exam and was awarded the Cordon Bleu Certificate, with honors.

The family's next move was to Tokyo where Annie studied for six months at the feet, (literally) of Kiyoko Konishi, the celebrated Japanese cooking instructor and TV personality. Annie made several appearances assisting Konishi-san on her weekly Japanese TV show. Regular trips to Tokyo's wholesale food markets and to the extensive food halls in major Japanese department stores broadened Annie's understanding of Asian ingredients and both traditional and 'westernized' Japanese cuisine.

A move to Singapore followed. This time around, Annie decided that she would be the teacher rather than the student, and started her Singapore Cooking School. Annie's students came from many nations: South Africa, Australia, Hong Kong, Canada, Malaysia, Singapore, the USA and the Philippines. The focus was on successfully creating *Elegant, Delicious* meals using straight-forward recipes that required no specialized culinary training or complex processes. At each session, Annie's students worked as a group to create a complete meal and then sat down together for a dinner with complementing wines. From the outset, Annie's school was completely booked with a steady waiting list.

Finally, Annie and her husband returned to their pre-revolutionary farm house in Massachusetts where she started to write *Annie's Elegant, Delicious Cooking*. Her writing was interrupted by a short assignment and relocation to Frankfurt, Germany where she prowled the restaurants and food markets around the country and added more knowledge of German regional cooking and specialty baking to her extensive, in-country experiences.

Springing from her life-long adventure with the pleasures of cooking, Annie has created a series of books that cooks at every level of experience can use to create *Elegant, Delicious* meals.

Index

hors d'oeuvres

THIRD IN THE SERIES: *ANNIE'S ELEGANT, DELICIOUS COOKING*

Made in the USA
Charleston, SC
27 December 2013